SECRETS OF
SENSUAL
LOVEMAKING

SECRETS OF SENSUAL LOVEMAKING

How to Give Her the Ultimate Pleasure

Tom Leonardi
with Arthur Gross

A DUTTON BOOK

DUTTON

Published by the Penguin Group
Penguin Books USA Inc., 375 Hudson Street, New York, New York 10014, U.S.A.
Penguin Books Ltd, 27 Wrights Lane, London W8 5TZ, England
Penguin Books Australia Ltd, Ringwood, Victoria, Australia
Penguin Books Canada Ltd, 10 Alcorn Avenue,
Toronto, Ontario, Canada M4V 3B2
Penguin Books (N.Z.) Ltd, 182–190 Wairau Road, Auckland 10, New Zealand

Penguin Books Ltd, Registered Offices:
Harmondsworth, Middlesex, England

First published by Dutton, an imprint of Dutton Signet, a division
of Penguin Books USA Inc.
Distributed in Canada by McClelland & Stewart Inc.

First Printing, August, 1995
1 3 5 7 9 10 8 6 4 2

 REGISTERED TRADEMARK—MARCA REGISTRADA

LIBRARY OF CONGRESS CATALOGING-IN-PUBLICATION DATA:
Leonardi, Tom.
    Secrets of sensual lovemaking : how to give her the ultimate
pleasure / Tom Leonardi.
        p.   cm.
    ISBN 0-525-93983-0 (acid-free paper)
    1. Sex instruction for women.   2. Women—Sexual behavior.
3. Female orgasm. I. Title.
HQ46.L43   1995
613.9'6'082—dc20   94-47136
                                                 CIP

Printed in the United States of America
Set in Times New Roman and Gill Sans

*This book is dedicated
to those who want
to share a deeper
connection with the one
they love.*

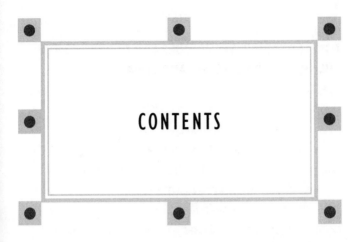

CONTENTS

CONTENTS

CONTENTS

NEW SEX?

In July of 1993, I was talking with Tom Leonardi on the telephone, and he mentioned that he was "doing this new thing to women, and it's driving them crazy."

"Yeah, new—right!" I kidded him.

"No, really," he said. "I'm doing this *new thing,* and women are going completely insane from it. It's unbelievable!"

"Are you serious?"

"I'm telling you—it's *unbelievable.*"

Tommy and I have been friends since the first day of high school, in 1979. And ever since then, he and I have spent *a lot* of time discussing women and his sexual escapades.

Tommy has been very "successful" with women. And over the years I'd heard dozens of his stories—and had been impressed many times.

But never had he boasted that anything was "new."

"Tommy, you're serious . . . ?"

And Tommy said, "Art, I'm telling you—this is completely different."

"Can you explain how to do it?"

"No problem."

"Let's write a book about it!" I figured maybe—just maybe—there was something to this *new* kind of sex.

I was skeptical, but I figured at the very least I'd get to spend a lot of time talking with Tommy about sex, and we did that all the time anyway.

So we got together at my sweet little grannie's house on Long Island, and for three days I kept asking him, "And then what?"

And for three days he kept answering, until finally Tommy Leonardi had nothing left to say about the topic of sex.

It was as if Old Faithful had run out of steam. (Ask anybody who knows him. Tommy is *always* ready, willing, and able to talk about sex!)

I came back to California with Tommy's step-by-step description of the technique he uses to produce ejaculating G-Spot orgasms in "eight out of ten women" with whom he tries it.

From the intimate details Tommy used to describe the process, this technique seemed to me like it might be the real thing. The only problem was that I didn't have a girlfriend at the time, so I couldn't try it out.

Instead, I gave The Technique to one of my roommates. He read it *quickly* and said he'd try it out with his girlfriend.

I was thrilled when he told me that, not only did it work just the way Tommy explained, but *neither my roommate nor his girlfriend had ever experienced anything like it before!*

When I finally got to try out The Technique personally with a woman, I was so anxious that I skipped a lot of steps and went right to touching her G-Spot.

The result was that the woman did not have an ejaculation. However, she did confirm that the way I was touching her was "COMPLETELY DIFFERENT," and that she had never felt a sexual sensation like it before.

But a week later, after I had reviewed the technique, not only did she again have "completely different" orgasms; she also ejaculated over and over.

She was so thrilled that she insisted we call and thank Tom Leonardi immediately at his home in Philadelphia—although it was 3 A.M. on the East Coast!

Everyone I know who has read the book and tried The Technique has confirmed that this is a NEW EXPERIENCE.

They also say that when they're having this new kind of sex, *they get more turned on and sexually stimulated* than they've ever been before in their lives.

What follows in the pages of this book is everything you need to know in order to join what many people are already calling "The Sexual Revolution of the '90s."

Now the rest is up to you. Read on and enjoy! And share what you learn with someone you love.

—ARTHUR GROSS
Venice Beach, California
September 1994

SECRETS OF
SENSUAL
LOVEMAKING

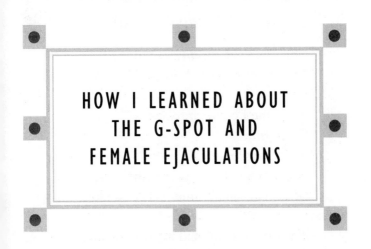

HOW I LEARNED ABOUT
THE G-SPOT AND
FEMALE EJACULATIONS

I was an astounded witness of G-Spot orgasms on two random occasions.

The first time, I met a woman at an art opening, and the attraction between us became obvious. The next day, when we spoke on the phone, it didn't take long for us to get into a discussion about sex. It was at this time that she told me that she was, as she called it, a "squirter."

I said, "Wait, I think I know what you're talking about. Do you mean that you have squirting orgasms? That when you come, liquid flows out of you?"

"No," she said. "It *flies* out of me."

My interest piqued, I pressed on: "What causes this?"

"Any time I come, it happens."

"Every time?"

"Every single time."

"Every single time you're with a man?"

"No, every single time. Whether alone, or with a man."

At this point I still had many questions. Instead, I asked her a single one: "When can I see you?"

The next thing I knew, she admitted to me that she was actually touching herself right then, while we were on the phone (as I had suspected by the urgency of her breathing). "Do you mind?" she asked.

"Please continue."

Within a minute, I could tell that she was coming. What was different about this particular orgasm was that her voice and her breathing seemed to be more than just an expression of her pleasure; they actually seemed to be a necessary—almost undeniable—release.

She told me that she had ejaculated as she came. Being male, I pictured a small amount of a white, creamy substance had just left her body. But to be sure, I asked what the substance felt like.

"It's really hot, and very wet," she said.

"And creamy?"

"No," she said. "It's nothing like semen, if that's what you're wondering."

"How much of it is there?"

"A heck of a lot more than any male orgasm has ever produced. But you'll have to see it to believe it!"

The next day, at her apartment, I enjoyed the single most erotic experience in my life (up to that time, at least!). We didn't even have intercourse. Ultimately, all it took was for me to touch her clitoris or the upper inner walls of her vagina, and she came *and* ejaculated over and over again.

The difference—aside from the obvious liquid—between her orgasm and any other woman's orgasm I had ever experienced was that I felt something unusual—yet very erotic—in and around her vagina.

To call what I had felt "contractions" would be an understatement. In the past, when a woman I was having sex with came, her contractions might have ranged from unnoticeable to somewhat discernible. But this woman's vagina *convulsed.*

Just before her orgasm, the inner walls of her vagina expanded, closing inward and creating an incredibly tight feeling around my fingers. I had to concentrate on keeping my fingers inside her, be-

3

cause if I had let them relax, her muscles would have pushed my fingers right out of her.

As I touched her clitoris, I could even *see* her convulsions: Between contractions, the opening to her vagina would actually increase in size. I could actually look in and see the movement of her inner walls.

It was always after these movements that she ejaculated. And again I noticed her unique breathing and vocal signals (like the ones I heard the day before, on the phone) when she came.

I was amazed at the very specific qualities of her sounds. In the past, I had heard many distinct styles of orgasmic vocalization: the moans, the groans, the panting, the swearing, and the typical breaking of the third commandment, "Thou shalt not take the Lord's name in vain." However, this woman's sounds of pleasure seemed uniquely bound to the fact that she was ejaculating.

She wasn't simply expressing how she was feeling; she was exhibiting a necessary release of something deep within. And, unlike other women who can be quiet if the situation demands silence, there was no way (and I confirmed this with her later) for her to control any of the sounds that came out of her mouth (and I'd bet her neighbors would agree with me).

As I left her apartment, I felt like an extremely lucky man. The sex studies I'd read said that this ejaculatory phenomenon occurs in fewer than 1% of all women, and that there's no way to know who will and who won't, or who can or who can't.

At that time I was right; I had been extremely lucky. As I found out over a year later, she was one of the 1% of women who automatically ejaculate with every orgasm. I didn't do anything special to her—that was just the way she would orgasm.

SALLY

Two years later I became involved with a young woman named Sally. Completely naked, in bed together for the first time, I felt a movement within her vagina that I immediately recognized.

Up to this point she had already achieved a "conventional" orgasm, mainly from me caressing her clitoris with my fingers and mouth. But about half an hour after that, as I held her close to me, with her head on my shoulder, in a position that was more *intimate* than sexual (I'll go into this important distinction more fully in a later chapter), I slid two fingers into her vagina and slowly massaged its upper wall.

I felt those same slow, almost deliberate expansions of the vaginal walls.

As with my previous G-Spot lover, I had to be sure to hold my fingers inside of her, because the movements of her muscles created a very tight squeeze within.

At the same time, I noticed she held me closer to her. She seemed to be asking for something with her body language—not just a hug, but almost a reassuring embrace.

I became extremely aware of not just the movements within the vagina but also the way her body seemingly desired me to be wrapped snugly, yet not too tightly, around her.

I continued to touch the interior of her vagina with my fingers, paying special attention to how she reacted as I varied my motion.

Suddenly, a slow, expanding convulsion pushing against my fingers let me know what was about to happen.

Her vagina instantaneously became extraordinarily wet—wetter than I thought possible, for she was already completely flooded inside. Yet she had not come.

Her muscle movements felt exactly the same as my lover's vaginal movements had two years before.

Seconds later, as she came, a hot, wet liquid shot out from deep within her.

I continued to touch her in the same way for several minutes longer. In that short period of time, she came in exactly the same way three more times.

Letting her catch her breath, I continued to hold her snugly in my arms. She looked at me in a curious yet bewildered way; she was astonished by what had just happened.

"Awesome," I whispered.

She just stared at me.

"You do realize what happened just now, don't you?" I asked her.

She stared and nodded.

"You did feel liquid shooting out from inside you?"

She nodded again.

"Has this ever happened to you before?"

At last she spoke. "No. Never."

I sensed that she might actually be a little freaked out by what her body had just done.

"You know, some other women do this, too," I assured her. "But you don't realize how lucky you are. From the few articles that I've read on the topic, they say that less than one percent of all women can do this. That's why you're so lucky."

"But why am I *lucky*?" she asked. "If other

women can come but not make it as wet as I did, it doesn't mean that they're not having orgasms. It's not like they're feeling anything different."

"Compare what you just felt to any orgasm you've ever had before in your life. Wasn't it intense? *Much* more intense?"

"Yeah, you're right. But in the past, not all of my orgasms were the same intensity."

"But were any as intense as this?" I asked.

She thought about it. "No. Not at all."

"See how lucky you are," I said. "You're one of that one percent of all women who can come like that."

But I didn't realize how wrong I was.

While I thought myself fortunate to have another lover who could do this, I later learned that while the first lover *naturally* ejaculated during orgasm, this time *it was I who made this happen with Sally.*

Over the next year, my relationship with Sally evolved into more of a friendship than a love affair. But our infrequent intimate encounters included conventional and ejaculatory orgasms as we continued to experiment and have fun with this novel and incredibly exciting aspect of female sexuality.

At the time, though, I still assumed she was one of that special 1% who had the natural inclination and physical capability to achieve an ejaculatory orgasm.

Then I met Joanna.

JOANNA

Joanna was an incredibly beautiful forty-five-year-old woman whom I had met at a department store. Aside from having an incredible body, she was also incredibly orgasmic.

The first two times we made love, she seemed to have an infinite capacity to orgasm. She would come while I stimulated her vagina inside or out, with either my fingers, tongue, or mouth. She also came easily and often during intercourse.

However, during our first two times together, the thought of an ejaculation did not occur to me because she didn't give any hint as to her ability to have one. In fact, up until this time I never thought about a female ejaculation with any woman because I assumed the odds were too great against my finding any more women with that ability; I figured that, if I happened to, I would be a *ridiculously* lucky guy!

The day after our second night together, Joanna and I spoke on the phone about sex. She told me that when she was in her mid-thirties she had an incredible series of ejaculatory orgasms.

"Do you have them anymore?" I asked.

"Oh, I *still* have them. In fact, I've had them recently."

"Well, unless I missed something, you didn't have any with me."

"Oh," she laughed. "When I say 'recently,' I mean I've had these orgasms by myself."

"You can only have them by yourself?"

"No," she said. "I could have them with you."

"You could? Great! So why haven't you?"

"I have to be more comfortable with you."

"More comfortable?" I interrupted. "You already seem about as comfortable with me as you could possibly be."

"Why do you think so?"

"How could you not be comfortable with me if you're having countless orgasms in every way and position possible?"

"It's difficult to describe," she said. "But it's absolutely the case. Just keep in mind that I need to be more comfortable with you. I can't guarantee that I'll ever feel comfortable enough with you to have it happen, but I think there's a good chance with the two of us—considering the way we already get along."

Of course, there was still one other question I had to ask: "So, when you're alone, you can do it by just touching yourself?"

"No," she said. "Actually, I don't touch myself with my hand. I have a special toy."

"What makes this toy so special?"

"It allows me to reach a nook deep inside me that would be difficult for me to reach comfortably with my fingers. I *could* touch it with my fingers, but the angle would make it impossible for me to sustain the rhythm and pressure necessary for me to come."

"And this toy makes you explode? How about other parts of your vagina?"

"No. Only that nook will make it happen."

She spoke very specifically about where she touched herself and how. I knew that this was something I'd have to keep in mind if she was ever going to ejaculate with me.

Also, her insistence upon being more comfortable prompted me to compare our sex with the ejaculatory sex I had had with Sally.

Sex with Joanna had been very hot, but it was

a purely *sexual* experience, with very little true intimacy involved. With Sally I was more tender and had spent a lot of time holding her close against my body.

Because Joanna was an older woman, I thought she would be perfectly comfortable having hot, raw sex with me—and she *was* quite comfortable. But I now thought that if I gave her more caring, intimate attention, she would then feel that extra level of relaxation and trust necessary to finally let it "flow."

The next time I was with Joanna, it worked out exactly as I had hoped. Instead of just ripping off our clothes and diving onto each other, I spent more time appreciating all parts of her body—not just with my fingers, not just with my hands, not just with my mouth, but with all parts of my body against hers.

I could feel the difference in her immediately. Her body language—the way she moved toward me, longing to be held—was reminiscent of Sally's movements.

I then began to gently massage the upper wall of Joanna's vagina, envisioning the movements that she might have used with her toy as well as the way I had touched Sally.

Within minutes I felt that now-familiar expansion of the vaginal walls. But unlike Sally, who had clutched me tightly against her when this happened, Joanna hugged me gently. It was obvious that what was happening to her was a familiar sensation.

I felt a sudden rush of extra-wetness in her vagina surrounding my two fingers. And about thirty seconds later, she let out an urgent shout as her ejaculatory juices squirted from deep within her.

I continued to touch Joanna in the same area and she just kept flowing.

She kept coming over and over and over again, for what seemed like an hour (but was probably closer to twenty minutes).

Finally, she asked me to stop, explaining that it was becoming so overwhelming that she was afraid she might pass out.

I removed my fingers and held her close.

It was at this moment that I began to wonder if my earlier conclusion—female ejaculations were limited to a special 1% of all women—was correct, or if perhaps it wasn't so limited an experience as people actually believed?

I recently asked Joanna if she could describe what it feels like to ejaculate. This is how she described it: "There are different kinds of orgasms, and they can all be nice in their way; but what we're talking about here is the ultimate."

DONNA

Donna was a friend and occasional lover in whom I often confided my sexual experiences.

I told her about what happened with Joanna, and she said that she, too, had heard of women ejaculating but knew of none who had done this themselves. She, too, believed that it was something that happened to a rare breed of woman.

What I *didn't* tell her was that I now believed that far more than just one out of every 100 women could ejaculate during orgasm.

During the next night that I spent with Donna, I paid special attention to the areas inside her vagina that helped to create the ejaculations of Sally and Joanna. But more important, unlike previous nights with Donna, this time I held her in a similar fashion to the way I held the other women.

After a while I recognized the now telltale movements of the inner vagina.

Her insides swelled and released, as the other women's had—and it was obvious she knew something completely different was about to happen to her.

I sensed a bit of apprehension on her part, but I didn't want that to interfere with what I hoped was about to happen. So I not only held her but I also encouraged her softly, whispering, "I got you . . . I got you right here . . ." as I held her even more closely to my body.

Soon Donna ejaculated for the first time in her life.

She continued to come in this way repeatedly, holding *me* closer and closer.

I honestly never thought that a woman could hug that tightly—with so much strength and urgency.

I don't know when we stopped or why we stopped, but when it was over, I held her quivering in my arms and didn't say a word.

She, however, looked right into my eyes and said: "I have never felt anything like that before in my life."

Hearing those words amazed me. Bear in mind, I had been with Donna many times in the past, and her capacity to have very loud, passionate "conventional" orgasms previously seemed infinite to me. But before I could even appreciate what she had felt, she continued by telling me that she could not have stopped herself from coming once it had started, even if she had tried with all her willpower.

"What if you had concentrated really hard?" I asked. "Couldn't you have blocked it?"

"I had no control over it at all."

"Could you stop yourself from having a conventional orgasm if you concentrated hard enough on that?"

"Oh, yeah, easily," she said.

"But there was no way you could have stopped this from continuing once it started?"

"No."

"When did you know that you couldn't stop it?"

"Actually, I think I knew just about a minute before I came."

I had an idea. "Was that about at the same time that I said, 'I got you,' and held you closer?"

She paused to think about it and said, "Yeah. It was right about then. Was that why you said that to me?"

"No. I didn't know exactly what you were thinking, but there was something obvious to me in the way you were moving that something incredible— but perhaps inhibiting—was about to happen to you. So I guess I just wanted to reassure you—even though I wasn't quite sure for what reason."

I had learned from my experience with Donna that a *combination* of physical technique *and* psychological security were absolutely necessary in order for a woman to have ejaculatory orgasms. I next set about to find out whether I could achieve the same result with a woman with whom I had never been before.

JILL

Jill was a twenty-year-old junior at a local college. We had met in passing at the gym but had never really gotten to know each other. One day she walked me home after working out.

Once inside my apartment, we immediately started kissing deeply and passionately.

Later, we were lying on my bed completely naked. I touched and tasted nearly every part of her body and wondered how she would react to the type of vaginal touching that I had done with Donna, Sally, and Joanna.

At this point, I had absolutely no expectations of being able to achieve an ejaculatory orgasm for Jill, as I hardly knew her, and she had not expressed to me any familiarity with the concept during our conversation. In fact, I sensed in Jill a certain lack of sexual experience, if not sexual naivete.

But I wondered what would happen if I touched her that way. Would she feel pleasure even if she did not achieve an orgasm?

I was enjoying what we were doing together tremendously, but I thought that she was in no way a woman who was psychologically capable of an ejaculation.

As I held her close and caressed the inside of

her vagina deeply and tenderly, her reactions were surprisingly similar to the reactions of the other women.

At first she seemed to be enjoying what I was doing to her. I touched her like this for at least twenty minutes, and her reactions made it clear that she felt wonderful.

She held me close, and the depths of her vagina seemed to become even softer and wetter.

And later, she held me even closer as her interior muscles expanded.

I decided to continue my movements and see what would happen.

Though I did not expect her to achieve ejaculation, I still felt it was necessary to reassure her that what she was feeling was okay, and I told her so.

While her sexual arousal was both obvious and dramatic in its intensity, I sensed that her lack of recognition of these new feelings was restraining her.

But as I kept touching her and holding her and reassuring her, Jill's urgency kept building and building.

And instead of just moaning, she started to yell.

Then to my surprise, this sweet, soft-spoken young woman started shouting at the top of her lungs, "Fuck! Fuck! Oh, fuck!"

I held her closer. "Let it all go," I told her.

I knew she didn't know exactly *what* she was

about to let go of, but it was clear she knew something completely unexpected was about to happen to her.

She shouted the most curious combination of "Oh, no! Yes! Oh, no! Yes!"

"Yes or no?" I urged. "Yes or no?"

Her vagina suddenly became *completely soaked.*

My fingers became surrounded by a liquidy—not creamy—substance, as she started yelling, *"Yes! Yes! Yes!"*

And within seconds her whole pelvic area convulsed—inside and out—as hot liquid flew out from within her.

This went on for a few minutes, and she came over and over again.

When I finally removed my fingers and held her closer to me, Jill gave me one of the sweetest kisses I've ever had.

"You know, I've never felt anything like that before," she said.

"So, you've never had liquid fly out of you when you've come?"

She seemed confused. She looked at me for a second and said, "What do you mean?"

"Well, didn't you feel the liquid come out of you?"

"Yeah," she said. "Of course."

"Well, what don't you understand?"

"Aren't all orgasms like that?" she asked.

"Does it always feel that way to you?"

"I don't know yet," she said. "That was the first orgasm I've ever had."

I paused. "You've *never* had an orgasm before—and you think that all orgasms are like that?"

"They're . . . not?"

"No," I sighed. "Not even close."

DO YOU ENJOY SEX?

The overwhelming majority of men don't enjoy sex; they enjoy THE FACT that they're having sex.

If you don't enjoy sex, you can't be a good lover.

Most women complain about men not being good lovers. And a lot of women don't even know what a good lover is, since the chances of any woman having met a good lover are so slim.

A tiny minority of men actually enjoy sex in the same way that women enjoy sex. You very rarely hear a woman say, "I got laid." They don't avoid this phrase because it's unladylike or impolite; women rarely think in these terms. Women actually enjoy and *appreciate the experience* that they have during sex. Unlike men, they are not impressed with themselves due to the simple fact that they have had sex.

In contrast, when a man talks about a sexual experience, what's the first thing out of his mouth? It's not "What a wonderful time I had last night," or "What an incredible lover this woman is." The first thing out of his mouth is often a proud—"I got laid."

The fact that men get so little true enjoyment out of sex explains women's biggest gripe against men in bed: Men come too quickly. And why shouldn't they? If a man's ultimate goal is just to get laid, and he finds himself getting laid, of course he's going to come almost immediately. With his objective fulfilled, there really is no reason for him to continue, is there?

Furthermore, if a typical guy is spending two to three minutes inside his lover, it's no wonder why she would fail to achieve a climax during sex. If a man enjoyed sex—*really* enjoyed sex—he'd make the effort to find a way to prolong the experience. Instead, most men (be they twenty or seventy years of age) only last a bit longer than a seventeen-year-old boy having sex for the first time.

But a man *can* make it last as long as he *wants.*

He can do it for an hour straight—if he really *wants* to. As *fast* as he *wants* for as *long* as he *wants*.

If more men wanted to *enjoy* sex instead of simply *have* it, there'd be a lot more good lovers out there.

WHAT IS SEX?

For me, sex is any erotic contact with someone else.

This can be anything from a deep kiss to intercourse and everything in between, before, during, and after.

I don't enjoy anything more or less.

I love blow jobs. And I love intercourse. And I love going down on a woman. And I love making her have an ejaculation.

But I also love the reaction on my lover's face when I'm concentrating on a so-called "nonsexual" part of her body.

Try it and see!

UNLIKE MOST GUYS

Congratulations!

If you're a guy and you're reading this book, you're unlike most guys in that you probably care about women and making them feel good. You're showing that you have a true interest in how women feel.

Sure, you're going to get a thrill out of this book, but the fact is that a woman is going to feel a thousand times better than the guy does when she experiences a G-Spot orgasm. So you're obviously giving and unselfish when it comes to sex.

BETTER MONOGOMY
THROUGH BETTER SEX

Although the techniques that follow have been used successfully by couples who don't know each other very well, one of the goals of this book is to help monogamous couples enjoy their sex lives more and thereby enjoy their relationships more.

Happy cats stay at home!

Monogamous couples in long-term relationships should be sure to read the section specifically for them.

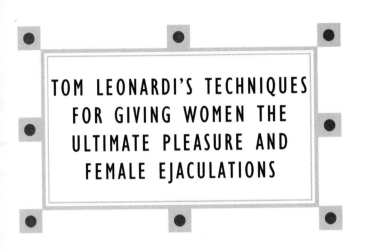

TOM LEONARDI'S TECHNIQUES FOR GIVING WOMEN THE ULTIMATE PLEASURE AND FEMALE EJACULATIONS

There are two components to my sexual techniques:

- Physical Aspects
- Psychological Aspects

I will explain the actual touching part of the process first so that people can get an overall mental picture of what they will be doing. Many readers will be tempted to stop reading after this section. If you do, you will be making a big mistake! The psychological aspects are *essential*.

In fact, *if you do not combine the physical aspects with the psychological aspects discussed in this book, you will fail to produce the desired result:* G-Spot orgasms and female ejaculations.

PHYSICAL ASPECTS

What follows is a description of how I might make love to a woman.

I never make love to women the same way twice, but what follows is a basic description of what I do, what I'm thinking about, what I look for, and so on.

"Ejaculatory orgasms" and "conventional orgasms" are different, and they require different techniques when a woman attempts to have them for the first time. It's often easier for a woman to have a first-time conventional orgasm while masturbating than it is to have one with a man. A first-time ejaculatory orgasm, however, is easier for a woman to achieve with a lover's assistance.

Comfort is the key! Once she learns how to have an ejaculatory orgasm, a woman can then have one standing, lying down, or in any position she feels most comfortable in. But first timers should try lying down on their backs on something soft, either a bed or a favorite couch. It should be flat and comfortable.

You should both be naked, with the man lying next to the woman.

You have to be absolutely comfortable with her entire body, and she has to be just as comfortable about having any part of your body touching hers. She will be this comfortable if you pay attention not only to the obvious hot spots—breasts, clitoris, anus and the like—but to *every* part of her body.

Have you ever touched her lips with your fingers?

Have you ever felt—not just touched, but really felt—and appreciated the texture of her ears?

Try running your fingers across her forehead, up through her hair, back down toward her neck. She'll love that.

You may ask yourself at this point, what does running your fingers through a woman's hair have to do with her having an ejaculatory orgasm?

A woman will not have an ejaculatory orgasm unless she is absolutely comfortable with you. Even a woman who is capable of having twenty conventional orgasms in a row with you may not necessarily be comfortable enough with you to have a single ejaculatory orgasm.

So you have to do more than just turn a woman on. You have to create a state of high arousal—and desire—and a willingness to let you do anything you want to her body. She has to know—at a core level—that there is nothing you will do that she will ever object to.

You want her to feel that nothing will hurt her, nothing will harm her, that you'll do nothing she'll regret.

You may want to try kissing her eyes (when they're closed, of course) very lightly, just barely touching the lids.

With every woman it's different, so you shouldn't have a checklist or routine when you're going to bed. It can't be mechanical.

After you're both naked, though, you might even want to treat her as if she still has her clothes on. Just because a woman's naked doesn't mean you should immediately dive between her legs—at least not every time. Pay attention to those parts of her body that women are used to having attention paid to when they are dressed:

Touch her hair.

Her shoulders.

Up and down her forearms.

Hold her hands. It's amazing how many people will hold hands walking around in public but will never hold hands in bed. Holding hands is incredibly important. When I make love to a woman, sometimes I can be on top of her and inside her, and I'll be holding her hands; not to pin her down, not to dominate her, but to let her know that a competent, caring person is there with her.

Don't be afraid to hold her hands or hug her at any point during your lovemaking.

Treat every woman the same way you would treat somebody you've known and loved for years.

Don't fake emotions, but love the fact that she's with you and you're with her.

Love the whole event.

Kissing is very important. If you kiss someone and you really enjoy kissing that person, then just keep kissing her. There's not a woman alive who doesn't love—if not long for—kissing.

Lovemaking should not be sequential. Don't follow a checklist or a set sequence of events.

You might go down on somebody and then figure, "We're gonna have sex."

No! Kiss her breasts, kiss her mouth. This might even confuse her. She may be used to a sequential approach. But women will go with whatever you want if it's obvious you're not pushing them through a sequence. She may say she wants to have sex with you after you've gone down on her, but she's not going to complain if you kiss her instead.

You never do what the woman wants until you're actually trying to make her achieve orgasm. And we're not there yet. We're still in the preparation phase.

At first stay away from her legs—they're below the waist, and any touching below the waist includes obvious implications that you don't want to deal with yet.

Turn her over on her stomach and run a finger up her spine while you kiss her.

Kiss her back. Not the spine, but the muscles immediately to the left and right of the spine, like you're giving her a massage with your lips.

There's no time limit on this initial foreplay; don't rush.

At any point you can go back and repeat a technique; there are things you shouldn't do before others, but once you've done something you can always go back and do it again.

EYE CONTACT

I love keeping my eyes open during all stages of lovemaking.

When looking at a woman's eyes, don't just look *at* her eyes—look into her eyes. What's the difference? The look of a lover who is turned on by and relaxed with you will be a look that nobody else has. All of a sudden the person will appear to be physically closer to you, even though neither of you has moved an inch.

People tend to close their eyes as they're getting turned on. Tell her, "Look at me." This will turn her on even more, because she'll see what you're doing and the look in *your* eyes while you're doing it, and neither of you will be able to subconsciously deny what you are doing.

I cannot stress enough the importance of watching and looking during all phases of lovemaking. Time after time, just looking deeply into the woman's eyes during any stage of lovemaking will suddenly increase her *and my* erotic state.

BREASTS

Before you touch a woman's breasts, run your hand along the skin from her neck to the belly button without making any contact with the actual breast—it builds anticipation.

Then caress her just to either side of her breasts, making them move with the movement of your fingers on her skin; this will create sexual arousal and vibration in the breasts.

If you're kissing a woman's breasts, don't just kiss them, don't just suck them—feel them. In fact, *don't* suck them, *don't* kiss them at first; just *feel them with your mouth,* and you'll end up naturally kissing and sucking them. She'll enjoy that ten times as much.

If it's possible, bring her breasts close enough together to kiss both nipples at once. Touch the nipples to each other, if you can.

Bring the nipple close enough to her mouth so that you can kiss her mouth and her nipple simultaneously.

Or let her kiss her own nipple while you kiss around her mouth. This is not necessarily an exclusive function of breast size—while this may not work with small breasts, not all large breasts will be able to accommodate a woman kissing her own nipple either.

Sometimes I squeeze women's breasts as if I'm trying to milk them, and they love it. This does not mean you should emulate a farmer milking a cow's udder! Massage them one at a time. Feel the nooks and crannies inside. Some sections are firmer than others. Imagine that there's liquid in there, and you're gently trying to massage it out. Don't hold the breast at the nipple. Feel the base of it with one or both hands, gently pushing into it, pushing that imagined liquid forward, slowly, a quarter inch at a time, all the way up to the nipple and then up the nipple and then through and up to the end of the nipple. You'll be a hero in your lover's eyes!

LEGS

You might not see an obvious connection between a woman's legs and her ability to have an orgasm, but keep in mind how much muscle mass is in our legs—and how much tension is normally in those muscles.

You want her legs to end up in a complete state of relaxation. Her upper body already is.

If you want to touch her vagina at this point, she will probably not object—if she hasn't asked you already. What she is not likely to realize is that the lack of relaxation in her legs is being masked by the state of arousal in the rest of her body. Most people at this point would probably have sex leading to a conventional orgasm. But we're not settling for that.

Kiss those legs!

Massage them.

Release the tension in the muscles. We stand on our legs all day. They support their own weight as well as the rest of our body, so give them the extra attention they deserve.

I like to include the buttocks as part of the legs. If you're massaging the legs, you should be massaging the buttocks as well. Also massage the hips and the sides of the buttocks and the backs of her legs. Treat the backs of her legs and her buttocks as one long entity. Do not think of them as separate from one another.

Give those cheeks a firm but not forceful squeeze. This action pulls the skin and muscles in the vaginal area, thus arousing more than its share of interest from the vagina. To make sure that this is actually happening, picture it happening in your mind as you're doing it. Picture the skin and the muscles moving. Picture what's happening and the whole connection.

Remember, the whole body is connected. You can't think only in terms of mouth, breasts, vagina, and so on. Too many people think just about the obvious sexual parts without understanding that the areas surrounding the sexual organs have an unexpected (and not so subtle) effect on the sexual parts.

I'm not a foot person, but I do have a few words about feet. If you have any desire to kiss or lick someone's feet, go right ahead. Again, use the same care and appreciation with her feet as you have with the other parts of her body.

How much time should be spent on the legs? There are no rules. It's up to you to decide when she's relaxed. Use your instinct, get a feel for things, don't be afraid to make your own appraisal of how she feels at a certain time. This is part of being a great lover.

A great lover knows how his or her partner feels at all times.

I know a woman's legs are relaxed when she's lying on her back and her legs naturally lie open with her knees slightly bent—not spread-eagle, but open wide enough that you would have no problem reaching your hand to her vagina and touching it. In fact, I would never touch a woman's vagina unless her legs were open wide enough for me to touch it without touching either of her thighs.

FINE-TUNING POINT: It doesn't matter if you start with the front or the back of her legs, but you'll probably get best results if you conclude the relaxation of her lower body with attention to the front of her legs, with her lying on her back. I suggest starting with the front, going to the back, then working on the front some more.

With these relaxation techniques, you're making your lover feel comfortable. But more important, she's learning to trust you because of the adoring way you're touching her. And with a little practice and experience, you'll be able to see and feel the signs of *arousal* and *relaxation* your partner is feeling.

DECIDING WHEN TO TOUCH HER VAGINA

You do not *touch her vagina until she is both adequately relaxed and suitably aroused.*

IS SHE RELAXED ENOUGH?

RELAXED HOLDING

After you have touched and massaged and enjoyed all of the nonvaginal areas of a woman's body

AND you think she is relaxed and aroused enough to proceed to direct vaginal stimulation, take her in your arms and hold her.

If she is relaxed enough, a woman will almost always hold you close with her hands or put an arm around you, as if she doesn't ever want to let you go. You'll feel her sexual urgency in the way she holds you, and this urgency will only be possible when she's truly relaxed and trusts her lover completely.

She won't necessarily grab you, but before you go on to touching her vagina, you should put an arm around her or hold her in your arms. If she is sufficiently relaxed, she will hold you in such a way that you both feel completely safe with each other.

IS SHE AROUSED ENOUGH?

If she's relaxed, she'll hold you. But when she's aroused, there'll be an unmistakable wave motion in her hips and crotch, if not also in her stomach and thighs and chest.

You must recognize this wave motion in her; otherwise she's not aroused enough.

It's not necessarily grinding. It could be very subtle—a movement that she's probably not even aware of herself. Just the tiniest up and down or back and forth movement. But it's definitely a back and forth "wave" motion, and unless you feel it, she's not aroused enough to proceed further.

She is aroused and relaxed and you're holding her. She's exhibiting that wave motion with some part of her body. Now what?

It's almost time to touch the vagina.

But not just yet!

You're close, with you on your side, leaning toward her, and with her on her back. (I don't recommend that she lie on her side because it's not as comfortable as lying on her back, and COMFORT IS KEY.)

A little-known, yet key, sexual area on the woman's body is the area below the belly button but above the pubic hair (assuming she doesn't shave it!).

During sexual excitement, there's a buildup of blood in that area (below the skin). Gently massage it, as if massaging out a knot in a muscle. After a short while, you will feel less tension in this area.

Don't do it for more than a minute, because it will become too tender.

At this point, you might want to give her another kiss, stroke her hair, etc. . . .

Remember, you're not just with a body; you're with another person.

VAGINAL CONTACT

I recommend that you begin by reaching your hand down so that your palm and fingers are covering—but not actually touching—the whole vagina.

Bring your hand close enough for her to feel the warmth of it, but not the hand itself.

In most cases, she will immediately push her vagina up toward your hand. Do not allow her vagina to touch your hand! Sure, perhaps you can let some of the pubic hair or the skin just around the vagina graze your hand, but don't quite touch her yet.

After her body has heaved toward your hand a number of times, use two fingers—one on each side of the vaginal lips—and gently touch the warm, soft area surrounding the vaginal lips. GENTLY!

This will drive her absolutely crazy.

If she tells you at this point to touch her vagina, to put a finger inside her, DON'T DO IT!

If she doesn't tell you, ask her what she'd like you to do to her. And if she then tells you to touch her, inside or out, STILL DON'T DO IT!

Continue to stroke the area around her vagina, and as you do, move your fingers apart so that you spread her vaginal lips apart. This will not only move the lips, clitoris, and general vaginal area, but will also allow some of the wetness (which has been building within her all this time that you've been with her) to move around inside of her.

At this point, she'll be so turned on she may grab your hand and try to push your fingers on or in her. DON'T LET HER!

Or she may try to put her own fingers on or in herself! DON'T LET HER!

She may offer you a million dollars to do it. If she does, take the million!

Don't be surprised if your lover has a conventional orgasm at this point (or before) simply because of the amount of relaxation and attention you've lavished on her—not to mention the sense of trust you've established. But remember, conventional orgasms are not our goal! (There's nothing wrong, of course, with her having one or many of them at any time.)

HOW LONG SHOULD YOU TEASE HER LIKE THIS?

Tease her until YOU can't stand it anymore—which, by the way, will be a lot longer than the point at which she can't stand it anymore. She'll be going wilder than either of you ever thought possible.

FLATTEN OUT THE LIPS

Now bring your fingers together toward the actual opening of the vagina. Stop on the lips and spread both lips open, as if you are trying to flatten them out onto the skin you were just touching a moment ago.

Note: The size of vaginal lips differs from woman to woman, so you can't necessarily expect to lay the lips flat out to either side on all women. But the very movement will further stimulate the woman, so it doesn't really matter either way—it's the movement that you want.

Now that the lips are spread apart, put your palm on the whole vagina.

Cup the area with your hand so that your middle finger touches the flesh between her anus and her vagina, and the heel of your hand rests on or past her clitoris.

Don't just cup it by leaving your hand there; actually hold it! Apply enough pressure so that she can feel your hand moving against it. She'll let you know she feels it because she'll be moving against you. Hold your hand there and appreciate the warmth and texture of her natural wetness. With your middle two fingers, put extra pressure against that wetness so that some of it seeps between your fingers. It is with this hot, creamy strip between your two middle fingers that you will now glide your hand upward and gently entrap her clitoris.

At this point, don't be concerned with *her* pleasure—it will be obvious to you. Rather, concentrate on how the combination of her clitoris and the slit between your two fingers feels to *you*. You might even want to picture her clitoris as a tongue or a nipple gently licking between your fingers.

REGARDING THE CLITORIS

Too much attention is placed on the value of the clitoris with regard to orgasm. This is understandable when talking about conventional orgasms, but we're striving for heights far beyond what is known to be orgasmic by most people.

When operating in the realm of the G-Spot and ejaculatory female orgasms, try to think of the clitoris as just another very sexy part of the woman's body—it is not to be solely thought of as the "love button" or the "magic button." It is just one ingredient in the magic love potion.

REGARDING CUNNILINGUS

You might wonder why I haven't mentioned cunnilingus up to this point. I have stressed the importance of your lover's trust in the experience—the bond of relaxation you have achieved and will continue to enhance. The key word here is BOND.

Sure, cunnilingus makes many women relax, but as soon as you remove your arm from around her shoulders, you're merely making contact mainly with your face and her vagina. *You have now turned this lovemaking session into a purely sexual experience.* This breaks the bond of mutual relaxation and trust.

Now, don't get me wrong—there's always time for cunnilingus and other exclusively sexual experiences (including fellatio, for that matter, ladies!), and you should not be afraid to enjoy both (and enjoy them often). But right now, in the pursuit of your lover's first-time ejaculatory orgasm, it is imperative to preserve that physical bond of *intimacy,* not just a heightened sense of sexuality.

Perhaps a better way to understand this is to imagine that you were expecting a relaxing—not sexual—deep-muscle massage from a friend, lover, or even a masseuse. The best massages involve unbroken contact between the hands and the body. Try picturing yourself on the massage table: Would you rather have a continuous massage for thirty minutes, or have the masseuse start and stop every so often during the session? In either case, you'll feel better afterward, but you'd achieve a much higher state of relaxation if the contact with your body was continuous.

HOW EXCITED SHOULD THE MAN BE?

You may *think* that you'd be better off to not get too turned on—in order to stay in complete control of the situation—but the only way to maintain her absolute trust in you is for her to sense *your* high level of excitement.

Allow yourself to become excited. As your urgency level increases, so will your concentration toward what you'll be doing inside her with your fingers. This concentration level is very important, because the physical technique necessary for the creation of the ejaculatory orgasm requires—demands—a very keen sense of timing and feel.

I DO NOT RECOMMEND THAT SHE BE ALLOWED TO TOUCH YOUR PENIS YET.

She will probably want to. You will probably

want her to. But if she starts touching your penis, you might get too excited and . . . lose control.

THE "CRITICAL NOOK"

When you feel that *you* have derived enough enjoyment from the clitoris-between-your-fingers segment of this session—when you get to the point where you *have to feel what it's like* to put your fingers inside her—gently slide your index or middle finger inside her. Don't swish your finger all around—keep the pressure on the topmost inner wall, the area inside and right behind the clitoris. This is the famous G-Spot.

Just to be sure you know where it is, I want you to imagine, if you will, that you are standing face to face with a naked woman, with your middle finger touching her clitoris. Now, slide your finger down and into the vagina, and hook it around that bone you'll feel there, until your fingertip touches the area of the vagina directly in back of the clitoris. That's the place. G-Area would be a better name for it: The G-Spot is not one specific *point;* it's an area, a region at least the size of a nickel, possibly as big as a fifty-cent coin.

As you first touch this area, use your other arm

(the one you're holding her with) to pull her body closer to yours with a gentle hug in order to reinforce her trust in you and her belief in your masterful sexual technique.

You'll feel her move when you first touch her G-Spot, and your hug should coincide with this reaction.

With this hug, feel her body anew: her head against your head or shoulder, your hips against hers, your legs against hers.

Feel her breath—not only the air that comes from her mouth but also the rise and fall of her ribs and chest.

Also, from this point on, anytime there's an obvious increase in her state of arousal (in other words, every time she moans, yells, or screams) be sure to, again, reinforce her unconscious (but very important) knowledge that you are as close as possible and can be fully trusted. While being aware of her signals and reactions, you must concentrate mainly on what your finger is doing.

Rub this interior surface (behind her clitoris) in the very specific way that I describe here. From this point on, you should maintain *some* level of constant pressure on this surface until the end of the session. Your fingers should never completely leave the vagina until you're done; in fact, the tip of your finger(s) should remain at least an inch inside the vagina so as not to tease the exterior of the vagina anymore with the rest of your hand. Also, don't push your fingers so deep that they touch her cervix.

At first, rub her G-Spot with a very soft up-and-down motion, as if rubbing a soap bubble that you don't want to break. This should be a tease, and you should do it for about a minute.

Do not overly concern yourself with the pressure your finger puts on the other surfaces of the interior vagina at this point. We are only concerned with the amount of pressure put on the "critical nook" or G-Spot.

WHAT PART OF THE FINGER SHOULD YOU USE?

Do not use your fingertips; you do not want to scratch this surface with your fingernail. Use the soft pad of your finger, the part that gets inked for fingerprinting.

Then begin to apply greater pressure to your up-and-down movement, increasing gradually to the amount of pressure you'd use to write your name on a fogged-up window.

Make a mental note of how this surface feels against your finger—it should be very slippery and very smooth, yet somewhat firm to the touch, much like a balloon with olive oil on it.

If at this or any time, the surface begins to feel less smooth, or if you feel ridges or bumps, you should return to a softer touch.

This area of the vagina changes texture, much the same way that a nipple changes, though less obviously.

Note: Contrary to conventional wisdom, my "research" indicates that direct clitoral stimulation is not necessary for orgasm, and in fact I have found that directly touching the clitoris at this time will most often inhibit a woman from being able to achieve an ejaculatory orgasm.

As you continue to rub inside her, be very conscious of the muscles beneath the upper wall of the vagina. You will soon feel a slight, slow contraction. These contractions are not orgasms, since the typical conventional orgasmic contractions occur about a second apart. These contractions are spread apart by at least ten seconds, and are simply reactions to your touch.

It is at this point that you should insert another finger (either index or middle finger) into the vagina to reinforce the actions of your first finger. This would be another perfect time to reinforce the intimacy of the situation by hugging closer or nuzzling your lover.

Now that you have two fingers inside, gently

hook your fingers around that bony section of the interior top of the vagina, and familiarize yourself with it and the way it feels. It is at this point that one or many of the following movements will bring your lover very close to an ejaculatory orgasm. (Since no two women are exactly alike, it is necessary to know *all* of these techniques. All of them will make her feel like a million bucks. But the right combination will make her feel like she could afford to pay off the national debt.)

1. Without moving your fingers up and down much at all, rub her with your fingertips touching her vagina between the bony area and the cervix. There are two variables in this: pressure and speed.

   Begin with the writing-your-name-on-the-fogged-window level of pressure. But as you feel her urgency building, you may want to start rubbing—if not actually pushing—harder.

   The other variable in this technique is how fast you move your fingers. You can vary the speed from a very slow, deliberate movement to an almost vibrating type of movement—and everything in between.

2. Move your fingers up and down in that magical nook, sliding in and out, but always returning to

the nook for the beginning and end of every movement. Of course, while moving this way, you can vary the pressure and speed as above.

But which kind of movement should you use the first time you try?

An excellent starting point would be to alternate between the specific-spot movement and the up-and-down movement described above. In each case, it is absolutely a *must* to move slowly at first, with no more than moderate pressure.

Be very aware of your lover's reactions.

See what she likes more, 1 or 2.

Alternate from one to the other, or even incorporate them into a third variation:

3. Slide your fingers in and out while lingering for a second or two on the magic nook.

Continue doing any or all of these techniques until you begin to feel muscle contractions that are very drawn out and deliberate.

It will feel like the inside wall that you are touching is expanding inward, suddenly creating an extremely snug fit around your fingers.

It will usually contract and expand again.

Sometimes it will expand outward past its original starting point, as if the vagina had grown much bigger and wider, or as if the vagina itself were filling up with air.

The main thing is to realize that these con-tractions are an absolute and positive sign *that an ejaculatory orgasm is approaching.*

It's possible that in the past you may have felt something similar to what I have described above while touching a woman inside her vagina. In those instances you probably had her at this exact point of excitement. However she did not have an ejaculatory orgasm for one or both of the following reasons:

1. You did not continue with the physical technique I'm about to describe, and/or
2. She was not psychologically prepared (i.e. re-laxed, comfortable, trusting) for her ejaculation to happen.

Remember, as I stated earlier, a woman will in-stinctively know at this point that something is hap-pening to her body that is

unlike anything she's felt before

and

not something she will be able to control once she completely lets it go.

Therefore, her trust in you must be complete and unequivocal. She may not have ever felt quite like that with you before.

But she does now.

You may also feel other contractions and/or convulsions:

above and through her pubic hair, her entire vaginal area will be going wild, and her ass will feel like it wants to open up.

As far as her breathing is concerned, most women are breathing very heavily at this point, but that's the least of it.

Vocally, she could be saying almost anything. She could be yelling, screaming, moaning, cursing, and/or referring to the Almighty. But for all her vocal outpourings, her physical reactions are equally intense, if not as obvious. She will simply hold you closer, hold you tighter; you must return the hugs, because what she is really doing is making sure that you are there, closer than ever. It is at this point that she will be going from 99% to 100% trust in you. If she feels she can *fully* trust you, she will soon give herself over to the oncoming flood-rush of physical sensation.

Now you will probably want to increase the pressure/speed (maybe both) of your fingertips. It's a unique situation with every woman. Sometimes a woman will like it one way on Monday and another way on Tuesday. Trust your instincts and tune in to what she feels like. Enjoy what you're doing and enjoy it for what it is. Don't think about *if* or *when* she's going to ejaculate; just think about and enjoy what you're doing to her.

Don't ask her any questions—just keep reassuring her with words of tenderness like "I've got you" or "Come here" in an almost protective way. Remember, she's about to do something over which she has no control once it begins. And she knows this on either a conscious or a subconscious level, even if she has never experienced an ejaculation before. She may not know exactly what's going to happen, but she knows it's going to be something she's never felt before.

PRE-EJACULATION

As you feel these contractions, you may want to apply more pressure—but not necessarily consistent pressure. Squeeze, yet still caress, that nook and inner wall.

There will be one more sign of the impending ejaculation, and that is—incredibly enough—an absolute parallel to male pre-ejaculatory fluid. You will feel the entire vagina suddenly get VERY WET. Pre-ejaculatory fluid differs from normal vaginal lubrication in two ways:

1. It's more watery, not as creamy or thick as vaginal fluid. It's much wetter.
2. It suddenly comes up all at once. Almost instantaneously, the vagina becomes VERY WET.

She is now on the absolute verge of ejaculation. At this point, it is vitally important to give 110% effort—one last kiss, an extra hug. Then hold on tight, because she, and you, are going on the ride of a lifetime.

FEMALE EJACULATIONS

Here it is: the big show, the main event!

At this point, there is nothing else for you to do right. All you can do now is screw things up. So don't!

Continue touching and caressing her critical nook in the same fashion. You may apply a little more pressure. Or you might want to decrease the pressure and increase the speed. Whatever it is, just keep it going, because she's going to be coming real soon.

You may feel a contraction or convulsion deep inside her that practically pushes your fingers right out of her vagina. Don't take this personally! She's not trying to push your fingers out; her vaginal muscles are now completely beyond her conscious control at this point. So make sure your fingers don't leave her vagina.

Whether it's another ten seconds, sixty seconds, or a couple of minutes, she's literally going to explode from within. At the very least, her hot liquid will quickly seep out of her, running down her buttocks and off her body. But most likely, the liquid will physically fly from her vagina—2, 4, 8, even 12 or more inches away from her.

When will it stop? It won't, unless you want it to. As long as you keep touching her, she will keep contracting. And over and over again more incredibly hot wetness will fly from her body.

Her body may take a tiny break here or there, but you can easily make this continue for thirty minutes or even more. But don't become complacent. Continue to reinforce the psychological intimacy and trust with hugs and tender words. Even better, encourage her: Tell her to let it go; tell her you want more. As long as she knows that you're loving every minute of what she's doing, she will continue to let loose with the most fan-fucking-tastic orgasms of your lives.

If at any point she says, "Stop, I need a break," listen to her. Actually, it doesn't mean you have to stop completely; this may be an excellent time to slowly slide your penis into her, if she wants your penis in her.

Think about the movements you made within her with your fingers and try to replicate these movements with your penis.

She may start squirting again while you're inside of her!

You may have to be Superman at this point in order to not come yourself, especially if this is the first time that you've ever experienced this. But if you already appreciate the way a hot, wet vagina feels around your penis, try to imagine what a convulsing hot, wet vagina will feel like while it spews all over your penis and scrotum!

WHEN SHOULD YOU STOP?

If you're a typical guy, you'll probably stop when you come. Even if you don't typically get hard again quickly, you may not need to. This experience is so erotic, you may stay hard for a week.

Try to judge by the woman's reaction to what's going on—and by your own erotic needs.

PSYCHOLOGICAL ASPECTS

In addition to the physical aspects, unless you satisfy the woman's psychological needs she will not be able to have an ejaculatory orgasm. There are three keys to achieving the required mental state: trust, relaxation, and desire.

TRUST

First of all, it is important to understand that the trust I'm talking about here is not the elementary kind of trust required to get a woman to go to bed with you. The trust I'm referring to is the more sophisticated and advanced level of trust that will be required for a woman to allow herself to completely abandon control of her body while lying naked in your arms. Think about that.

Physical comfort is an important first step in achieving total trust. Without first establishing a comfortable environment in which to attempt the procedure, you might as well forget about succeeding at achieving an ejaculatory orgasm.

RELAXATION

Put some thought into finding a suitable location for your sexual experimentation. Is the place soothing? Does the environment feel safe? Or is the guy in the next car revving his engine?

Also put thought into getting your lucky lover in a good "mental place": Is she worried about a big presentation she has to make at work tomorrow morning? Does she have to be home by midnight to drive her baby-sitter home?

Chances are you'll get better results if you set up a special getaway weekend for you and your lover, one where you both can forget about the pressures of everyday life and can concentrate exclusively on taking sexual hedonism to new heights.

Unless she's completely relaxed, it ain't gonna happen.

DESIRE

People do what they want to do. They rarely do anything that they don't want to do.

In order for a woman to have an ejaculating orgasm, she must be willing to lose control of her body. If she doesn't lust after this orgasm enough to go completely wild for it, *you're not going to be able to make her do it.*

THE IMPORTANCE OF BEING NAKED

The importance of being naked cannot be stressed strongly enough when attempting to induce an ejaculatory orgasm in a woman for the first time.

When you're both naked, you're on equal ground. You're both equally vulnerable and equally exposed. But more importantly, clothes can create a physical distraction that can prove detrimental to the required levels of relaxation and trust when in pursuit of the elusive first-time female ejaculation.

Also, if a woman won't take off all her clothes with you, she's probably not anywhere near relaxed enough to have an ejaculatory orgasm. Likewise, the man must be naked in order to demonstrate his openness and trust with his lover.

LIFE AFTER EJACULATION

After a woman's first G-Spot experience and ejaculation, she will be capable of having ejaculatory orgasms in less demanding and/or precise circumstances.

Once she knows what her body can do, and after she's had some time to absorb what's happened to her, she can then experience the new orgasmic thrills in varied positions, with your penis as well as your fingers, and even while dressed or partially dressed.

She'll be able to do it standing up . . .

lying on her stomach or side . . .

while sitting or squatting over you . . .

in the bathtub . . .

on the subway . . .

or while talking on the telephone.

Just as a woman is likely to find it easier to reach a conventional orgasm after her first time, she will also find it easier to achieve ejaculatory orgasms once she is aware of her ability to do so.

EXPRESS YOURSELF

Learn to express yourself in words as well as sounds.

If you want to scream, scream.

If you want to yell, yell.

If you want to say "suck me" or "fuck me" or "kiss me" or "touch me"—say whatever the hell you're thinking of!

Everyone's heard "It's important to communicate in bed." But what does that mean?

Most people think that it's very important to sit down and discuss it. But it's not a matter of sitting down and discussing anything. More often, it's an unspoken discussion—using the language of love.

By the way, if you are going to actually discuss your sex life or the idea of trying out the techniques in this book with your lover, the worst place to do it is while you're lying in bed with her. It puts a lot of unneeded pressure on you both.

If you talk about it while you're walking around or at dinner, it may not seem appropriate, but it's really the best place because it will have a chance to sink in. Give it a chance to sit for a while and sink in, and it will probably pique the interest of both parties later on!

A SPECIAL NOTE TO
COUPLES IN LONG-TERM
RELATIONSHIPS

Couples who have been in long-term sexual relationships have many advantages working for them when utilizing this book's techniques:

- You're used to being naked together
- You're used to having sex together
- You have established trust
- You've probably tried all or many of the different positions and contortions in *The Joy of Sex* and other such books, and have a familiarity with each other's bodies and sexual tastes.

However, there may be distinct disadvantages working against you:

- You may have established sexual routines that are hard to break
- You may not like having sex with each other anymore
- You may have developed trust *issues* (a.k.a. lack of trust).

Follow the techniques in this book in order to break your old routines. Don't always do *exactly* what I do, but certainly do it the first couple of times; then experiment with each other to keep it exciting.

One of the reasons you bought this book (or your lover bought it for you) is to enjoy the sexual aspect of your relationship. Congratulations! The techniques you learn in this book may give you a much-needed and long-awaited return to excitement and fun in your love life.

Trust—or lack of trust—is a key element in the technique. Infidelities may haunt your past, but the kind of trust I'm talking about is more primitive and primal; does she trust you with her *life*?

Your woman must trust you with her safety and well-being; if she does, you're on your way to the main event; if she doesn't, it ain't gonna happen.

A man might wonder if he'll be able to utilize the techniques in this book without his wife or long-term girlfriend noticing what he's doing.

Impossible.

Most women have never experienced the pleasures of G-Spot stimulation, and it's a completely new, different, and powerful sensation for them.

So, since you're not going to be able to sneak it by her, you should talk about trying out some "new sex techniques" with your lucky female lover.

Remember, *don't discuss it in bed right before you want to try.*

Discuss it during the car ride to Las Vegas, and then wait till later that night.

Or discuss it on the way to brunch, or on the way to work, or *any* place, any time, except in bed right before you want to have sex.

Allow the idea to percolate so she can get used to it and get turned on by it too.

Remember, for most women this will be a *new sexual experience* and will be exciting to think about.

Your lover may want to read the book, and you could let her, but she'll have more fun if you do the techniques to her first and then let her read the book afterward. Most women require assistance in order to produce a first-time ejaculation, so there's really not much point in her reading the book first.

You might want her to read the testimonials later in the book, or you could read them to her. This will surely whet her appetite or intrigue her.

Hopefully, your lover will have heard or read about the book. She'll know how lucky she is that you want to try the techniques with her.

Ideally, your woman should be thrilled to try this and to just lie back and enjoy her first experience with a whole new aspect of her sexuality.

In reality, however, she may be afraid or apprehensive. You could remind her that female ejaculations are completely natural.

She might not ejaculate the first time; that's okay! It may take several sessions before she gets comfortable enough with the idea of letting go. Or she may never ejaculate, and that's okay too!

Women will enjoy the techniques described in this book whether or not they ejaculate. It's up to a man to instill a level of comfort and trust so that his lover is able to let go.

But remember, ladies, it's up to you to let go! Men can't do it for you!

Another point I'd like to make is that a lot of couples who have been together for a while take sex for granted. It's just seven pleasant minutes before going to sleep on a Saturday night.

That's the wrong attitude to take when trying out these techniques.

Make a special event out of your first experiences with the G-Spot. Make a day of it! Seriously. Drive out to the country, go for a walk in a state park, have a nice dinner at a romantic little restaurant, and check into a charming hotel. (Not one with paper-thin walls!)

Once you've learned how to use the techniques successfully, you've still got to make time for this expanded sexuality in your lives. The massage takes time, but you both deserve it. It's often more fun to give in life than it is to receive.

Now, a lot of couples seem to establish over time a silent set of rules about what is done—or not done—and by whom, in the bedroom. Your old systems of lovemaking can prevent you from being successful at what this book is all about. The man must be able to take control of the entire experience, and the woman must allow him to be in control in order for this to work.

She must trust that you know what you are doing, that it's all completely natural, and that its focus is exclusively on one thing: *her pleasure!*

Part of the problem may be that after a while

couples tend to view things as a single entity. You might have heard yourselves say, *"We don't like hot dogs,"* or *"That's not the way we do things."*

A woman's first G-Spot orgasm is something that only she can do. The man is just a tool in the process. Don't think in terms of "we"; think in terms of "she" and "her." *She* is going to love this. This is for *her* pleasure.

Sure, guys will find the entire experience extremely erotic and sexually stimulating. *But to be successful, a man must possess a single-minded determination to give her the ultimate pleasure experience.* Once she gets "there," you'll both be there. But she's got to get there first.

Lastly, I want you to think back to the beginning of your relationship (or to your first sexual experience) and remember when sex was new and used to be an adventure.

Perhaps one or both of you have experienced a yearning for newness and adventure in your sex life that prompted you to read this book.

Well, that's where you are again. You're at the brink of an entirely new and extremely exciting phase of your sexual life with one another.

Enjoy it!

And enjoy each other!

FINAL REMINDER TO MEN

Once you begin your quest for the female ejaculation, stick to the guidelines given in this book. At the same time, be ready to improvise!

It's going to be steamy and erotic and could be wilder than anything you and your lover have yet experienced.

Both of you will be dying for you to insert your penis in her vagina. She'll be grabbing you and moaning and imploring you to stick it in.

"Fuck me!" she'll be yelling. "Please put it inside me!"

Don't do it! Don't give in!

Remember your objective!

Hold out for that million-dollar offer!

Hold her! Encourage her!

Make it happen!

ADVICE TO WOMEN WHO CAN'T "LET GO"

My advice to women who can't "let go" enough to have an ejaculation is this:

- Trust your instincts—take a more naturalistic approach to life.
- Be honest with yourself. Women can be more honest with themselves than men can. They don't have this macho bullshit image to carry around with them.
- Be aware of your shortcomings, but don't dwell on the negatives. Try to build positive images.
- Don't be so hung up about the idea of wetting the bed. It's not urine. And it *will* dry!

This may not seem like much, but this simplistic approach has worked wonders for many people!

TESTIMONIALS

Following are transcripts of testimonials made by people who have experienced Tom Leonardi's techniques in the pursuit of G-Spot orgasms and female ejaculations.

DONNA, AGE 27

When it happened, it kind of scared me at first, because I didn't know what was happening. I exploded. It was a rush. It was a release, it was incredible. I didn't think it was ever going to happen again.

But it happened over and over and over.

I thought it was a particular spot that you were hitting, and sometimes it is, but it doesn't need to be.

The first time, it was definitely a certain spot that you were rubbing. And it kept happening over and over and over again. I mean *continuously*. I could have probably gone all night!

It was incredible that I just kept going and doing it and doing it and doing it. And the more I did it, the better it was.

And when it happens, it's like, oh my God—it's like heaven. And then you know you're doing it.

Compared to a regular orgasm, this is *much more* of a release.

What makes it happen?

It's a combination of things. Who you're with, what type of mood you're in, if you're connecting with the person.

Sometimes it will happen with a person, but then the next time it won't. And it's frustrating, very frustrating. You want it so bad and it won't happen, and it's more like you're trying too hard. And sometimes you're on the verge and you can't come, and you just want it so bad because it feels so good.

Do other guys know how to make this happen?

They don't. I think it's *me* now.

What do you mean by "now"?

I can't just make myself do it. But one time I was with this one guy—he didn't even have his fingers inside me. He rubbed his hand up against me and I just exploded.

Did you know it was going to happen?

A lot of times I don't know it's going to happen. But I know when I do it, because it feels so much better than a regular orgasm.

Why didn't it happen to you before I concentrated on making it happen?

Most of the time it's a pressure point—a certain spot. And then sometimes it's that I'm so caught up in the moment that it just happens.

But why didn't it happen before?

I didn't know how to do it. I never knew it could happen to me. I mean I knew it could, but I didn't think that any plain old, regular person could do it.

I always thought that it was these professional people—in movies—who could do it. I saw this movie one time, and it was about this woman who could do it. Before that, I never knew that a woman could actually come—that way—kind of like a man.

It takes a guy about twenty minutes to recuperate. But for me, sometimes there's one after another, and there's not even a pause. Several times I've lost count after nine or ten. And even if I was to stop, if we were done, within five minutes—I wouldn't even have to take five minutes—I'd be ready to do it again.

Really?

Yeah. It's so different with a woman.

Sometimes I really have to think about it. Especially when I'm with a person who doesn't know my body. But the combination of my trying too hard and his not knowing what to do can sometimes stop it from happening.

Do you tell guys before—about what's going to happen?

One time I was with my ex-boyfriend, when we had gotten back together, and it had been a long time since we had slept together. We were messing around and he had his fingers in me and I just completely exploded. And he just looked up at me—and he was stunned.

How long had you known him?

Eight years.

It never happened? In eight years?

Never. He just looked at me. He was a little pissed off, because this was a new thing, and I was the only person he had ever slept with, and he was the only person I had ever slept with, and then three years later I'm squirting all over the place. He was a little pissed—but he was excited because it had happened.

One time, though, he was going down on me, and I came in his mouth, and he totally loved it.

Really? What did he think about the way it tastes?

He was going down on me, and I don't know if he had his tongue inside me or just going around the outer edge, but it just exploded. And when he looked up, his whole face was covered, and it was dripping. And he looked at me and he was loving it and he kept doing it. He just kept doing it.

What does it feel like?

Everything tightens—the vaginal area—especially when you're trying to make it happen. You can feel it in your stomach. The more muscle tension that you have, the more you're going to squirt.

So you can actually make it squirt farther?

Yeah.

Wow. See, when a guy ejaculates, he has no control over how far it goes.

Yeah, but most of the time I'm on my back, so I have no idea how far it goes. But one time I was on top—I didn't have my fingers inside, they were just on the outside, and I was rubbing and I just exploded, and it ran down all over him.

Compare this to how it feels when you're urinating.

It's three times as hot as when you're going to the bathroom. When you're going to the bathroom, it's one stream coming from this one little tiny opening, and it's just concentrated. It's a direct stream that you can feel. If you were to stop, you'd know that you had stopped. But when you're coming and squirting like that, it's not a stream, it's a gush, just coming from everywhere.

Where is it coming from?

You know it's coming from your vagina, but it feels like it's coming from so deep inside you. You actually can feel it when you're about to—it's like this rush, and then all of a sudden it's coming out.

I can't stop it from happening—at any point. If it happens once, it's going to continually happen until we're done.

Can you do this alone yet?

No, I can't. Sometimes it just happens. Sometimes I really have to work at it to make it happen. And then sometimes I try to work at it, but it's just not happening.

Most of the times when I try to make it happen and it doesn't, it's because of the person I'm with and what he's doing to me or not doing to me. What the pressure's like, if he has his fingers in me, how far. Is he going in and out or moving in a circle or back and forth, just wiggling . . . or how fast he's going or how slow he's going.

What specifically works for you?

You go in, and put your fingers toward the front. They're in, and you move them toward me. Sometimes you need to use hard pressure; sometimes you don't.

How fast?

Most of the time, fast.

How long does it take before it happens?

Sometimes it doesn't take any time at all. And sometimes it takes a while—from a couple to twenty minutes.

JOANNA, AGE 45

I asked the gynecologist about it because I was curious about it. I wasn't able to find much to read about it. I was in my early thirties when it started. I had been sexually active for a long time before that, and it had never happened. I didn't know what it was. I hadn't read anything about it. I hadn't heard anything about it. I didn't know if I was some sort of freak of nature. I couldn't figure out why I couldn't find anything written about it anywhere.

So I asked [my gynecologist], and he didn't know anything about it, so he referred me to a female colleague of his. She said she had heard of it but that she didn't know very much about it either.

I finally searched out a book on the subject, and at last I was able to say, "Oh, yes. That's what happened to me." That book was called *The G-Spot.* It was my understanding that it was the stimulation of that spot that triggered the ejaculation.

It's kind of remarkable when you think about it. With as much as we know about anatomy, it's a mystery to me why it's not a part of normal sex education. So many people don't know about it.

How many other women do you know who have experienced this?

None.

Tell me about your first experience.

I was with someone I had been with for quite a long time. When it first started happening, he said it was me who was making the bed wet. I said I thought it was him, because I wasn't tuned in to the sensation of it.

It seems to me that it's kind of like a skill that you hone. I don't know why it first happened—if it was the position we were in, or the intensity, or the comfort—but when it did start to happen, and I became aware that it happened, I also noticed that there was a difference in the release and the feeling afterward. It's much more complete.

Once you begin to learn how to master it, you can help it come along and begin to learn how to work with it and not against it.

How did you master it? What did you have to do?

It's a very difficult thing to verbalize because ejaculatory orgasms, as you call them, are *so intense,* and they don't always happen.

It depends on who your lover is, how skillful he is, and how comfortable you feel with him. But I *can* do it when I masturbate. It's got to be a combination of factors.

Psychologically, it's a matter of letting the intensity go beyond what you normally can tolerate.

Tolerate?

You reach a level where you just go, "That's it." But what I'm saying is that there's a way to go beyond where you think, "That's it"—and kind of relax and just—everything inside settles, and it just goes and goes.

I'm definitely aware in my head what's happening, as well as what's happening in my body. In my head I can almost control whether it happens or not. I can hold it back or I can let it go.

What makes you decide to either hold it back or let it go?

I don't think it's a decision as much as sometimes I'm in the right state of mind. If I'm not in the right state of mind, it doesn't happen.

What does it feel like when it happens?

There's a release of fluids. And then the sensitivity is like you're all fired up. And then progressively it's much easier to do it a second or a third or a fourth time—once the gates have opened up.

It's like a passageway. Once that happens, and I've gone through that passageway, then I'm in another place—my body's in another place.

The important part is to get it to happen the first time. Once it happens, then it can happen 2, 3, 4, 5, 8, 10 times, whatever—that's super-easy.

The difficult part is getting it to happen the first time each time. But that first time is getting to that point; then once you get to that point, you're already over on the other side.

When you're on the other side—in terms of your control, what can you say about that?

I've never tried to have any control after that, because the effort is over at that point.

There's no effort anymore.

There's no anything anymore.

It just happens and you feel great.

So if it happens again and again and again—it just happens till you're totally exhausted, totally drained.

That's the great part.

MARY, AGE 26, GYNECOLOGY STUDENT

The thing I remember most about it is just feeling very strange. I felt numbness, tingling—I felt numbness around my mouth. I don't think that's so strange, because when you hyperventilate you experience peri-oral numbness, and I was definitely breathing fast.

That's what I remember most. I thought, "Holy shit,"—I felt really strange, and it kind of scared me. I felt very light-headed, but that would go along with the hyperventilating.

Why was that different from other sexual responses that you'd had?

I was kind of fighting the whole thing.

But then after I let go, it was almost like a man had come inside me and it was dripping out of me.

Where did the liquid come from?

Supposedly there's something like a female prostate gland.

Supposedly? Why hasn't medical science documented this?

Until recently, medical science hasn't given two shits about women's bodies. I'm going to be a gynecologist, and up until the first time you showed me how to have what you're calling an ejaculatory orgasm, I would have said: "What the hell are you talking about?" There's been no medical test case that I'm aware of.

BETH, AGE 36

The sensation that leads up to an ejaculatory orgasm is not unfamiliar. That's the deceptive thing about it. Unknowingly, I've been close to it before, and so have many women that I've talked to, and it seemed like a sensation that would naturally lead to something, yet it never went anywhere.

Why not?

Because neither the men nor I knew that there was any point to that kind of digital stimulation. The biggest obstacle to getting past the sensation and to the "ultimate orgasm" itself is that you have the definite impression that you've simply got to take a pee; that you can't go any further unless you do. However, as soon as the stimulation stops, the urge to pee is gone. Or if you try to go to the bathroom, there's little or nothing there.

So for me it was getting past my fear that the release I was seeking was just taking a pee.

The first time it happened, I was so worked up I was half crazy because I was convinced, when I was closest to letting go, that I was going to wet the bed. The guy I was with said, "Go ahead, wet the bed." And in fact, I cried out in desperation and frustration, "I can't do it." As soon as I declared this, I was able to let go.

When I read the physical techniques Tommy describes, I thought all that silly business about holding the woman was Tommy Leonardi's ego about the man being really needed in the process. But for me, I was absolutely out of control and felt as though I was falling through space, and holding on to my guy was the only way to stay in touch with reality.

I never really discussed sex before, but now I want to tell everybody about this; male or female, young or old. For some reason, this topic of conversation breaks all barriers. Some people don't know about it and some people do, but it's fascinating for both.

I'm so enthusiastic about this technique I want to tell the whole world.

TAMMY, AGE 24

The kind of sex you teach in your book is like a different door to go through.

I mean, it used to be that there was clitoral stimulation and penetration, and that's it. And when we would have sex, I'd always have to play with myself in order to come.

But now, if my boyfriend uses the techniques in the book, it strengthens the power of sexual intercourse.

How does an ejaculatory orgasm compare to a conventional orgasm?

It's another road.

It's completely different from a regular orgasm.

The first time you experienced it, did your boyfriend tell you what to expect?

He told me in the car that he had something he wanted to try, and he was excited to do it. He didn't really elaborate on it at all.

You didn't ask?

I asked, but he said he thought it was better if we didn't talk about it.

We checked into the hotel, and we were both really tired, so we lay down. He rested me on my stomach and told me to relax, and then he started kissing me and massaging me, and rubbing me, and touching me. And then he rolled me over, and I was aware that something different and new was going on, because it's not often that we'll start off sex that way.

So I rolled onto my back and he put his hand between my legs, and rested his chest next to mine, and put his arm around my shoulder, and then he started talking to me.

He said, "I want you to relax and go with whatever you're feeling, and it's okay if nothing happens. This may feel strange, but try to feel what you're feeling."

I was really relaxed because of what he said and how we were together.

We looked at each other, and there was a level of assurance from that.

He was touching me inside, and I was kissing his neck, and I kind of lost myself in feeling his body next to mine, and the feeling was different.

It used to be really hard for me to have sex.

As the feeling built inside you, how did you feel, physically? How did that feeling of coming differ from previous times when you were on the verge of orgasm?

In the past, when I was having what you call conventional orgasms, the feeling of coming was tension. It's a tight orgasm, whereas the feeling of these new orgasms is much more relaxed. It's more open.

It's relaxing during the whole time, not just at the end.

It's just like opening up.

It's a release.

It's never a tightness. I'm not really squeezing so much as I'm pushing.

I believe that there's a certain amount of finger stimulation that's necessary for me to ejaculate. If I stop him too early, and then we have intercourse, I'm not likely to come that way.

How has this new type of orgasm changed your psychological outlook on sex?

Amazingly. Before we knew about this, sex wasn't as much fun. I was too uptight about whether I would come or not, whether it felt good or not.

But no matter what, it always feels good when my boyfriend uses his fingers the way you instructed him to.

I'm automatically brought into the sexual experience, because the feeling is *so* sexual and so orgasmic. When he touches me like that, I just *know* I'm going to come.

I can relax with it and enjoy it and—this may sound like a stupid sweepstakes testimonial—but it made my sex life much more relaxed.

I'm no longer concerned about whether I will come or not.

Now I'm more free with sex. More open to it. I'm not as uptight.

I'm no longer frustrated with sex.

It's released the concern of "Can I come or not?"

What would you tell women who may benefit from this?

I'd tell them that at first it feels weird. You may feel like you're going to the bathroom, but you won't, and you're not.

Just close your eyes and feel it.

What would you tell men if they want to successfully use the technique with a woman?

The massage you recommended is a really good idea. Massaging around my lower back and my stomach was very relaxing and good.

The man should tell his partner—or even a woman could tell her female partner!—that they may feel something strange, but that it's okay, it's part of the feeling, and not to stop it.

The first time this may feel kind of weird, but that's what it is, and don't push it away.

Another interesting way of feeling the finger stimulation is for the woman to be on her hands and knees.

Sometimes my boyfriend lies on his back, and I go down on him—sucking his penis in a sixty-nine position—and he'll put his fingers inside of me, and I swear, I'll squirt in less than a minute.

I wouldn't recommend this position for the first time you try, because it's more comfortable to be on your back, and you have to feel it and learn how to do it the first time or the first few times.

Have you noticed any smell to it?

I think it smells like vanilla.

And one other thing: I think that these new orgasms are much like male orgasms. I mean, compared to how my boyfriend reacts when he has an orgasm, I feel like these orgasms are very similar.

Unlike the feeling with conventional orgasms?

Right.

What I really like about these orgasms is that I feel they're for me.

Maybe I was uptight about sex because I always felt like I was serving the man's needs.

Now I'm feeling like I get something out of sex too.

CLINT, AGE 29

The first woman I tried it with was an old girlfriend whom I hadn't seen in years. She was a very uptight corporate lawyer in New York City and not very trustful or sexual by nature, and I could tell that the new levels of heightened sexual awareness brought on by touching her G-Spot made her very aroused, but also very nervous.

I'll admit, I was too anxious to try touching the G-Spot to see what would happen and how she would react. I didn't follow Tommy's instructions at all. I didn't bother trying to relax her with massage or even establish any level of trust before touching her "magic nook."

The next day, she told me she didn't want to see me anymore.

The second woman I tried it on was another old girlfriend, but this one was a graphic artist in California, much more laid back and open sexually and emotionally. I told her I had read about new sexual techniques, and she seemed excited to try it.

Again, being anxious, I failed to heed Tommy's advice about relaxation and trust, and just plunged my fingers right inside her.

As soon as I touched her G-Spot she said this was "completely different."

And as I continued to touch her there, she became aroused to a state I had never before experienced with her.

Finally, after she had squirmed and moaned on the wall of pre-ejaculation for about ten minutes, she said, "I can't do it. You've got to stop. It's too intense."

I tried to convince her to let it go and let it flow, like Tommy says, but she just wouldn't do it. The bottom line was that we didn't have the level of trust necessary to get over the barrier of fear and insecurity, and after all the time we'd been apart, she probably wasn't relaxed or comfortable enough with me to let go in that way.

The third time I tried the techniques, I resolved to do *exactly what the book said,* especially the relaxation techniques, like massage, touching, treating the person like a person and not a sex object or experiment.

Luckily for me and my partner, we had begun a wonderful loving and trusting relationship. I didn't rush into trying anything with her, because I wanted to do it right and have it work the very first time I tried it with her.

Wow! I wish I had listened to Tommy from the beginning! Not only does my partner experience the ultimate orgasm, but I get turned on by the experience like nothing I've ever done before.

Conventional orgasms and "normal" sex are much more cerebral than this "new" kind of sex.

After she's been coming for five or ten minutes, I find us both saying things and making sounds and physical movements like we've never done before.

She says it's like a drug, and completely different than any kind of sex or sexual feelings she's ever had.

Now, although we don't have G-Spot sex every time we have sex, my girlfriend is able to have squirting G-Spot orgasms whenever we try to do it.

Looking back over my several attempts and experiences, I'd say there are a couple key points:

Read the book carefully, if not several times. This is a very subtle area of sexuality, and you want to know as much about it as you can. As you become experienced with this new sex, you'll see that *everything* you need to know is contained in this book.

Comfort really is the key! The woman must be comfortable and relaxed. A full-body massage is a must for first-timers and a great overall sexual aid for both the man and the woman. Massage those legs! Rub that butt! Lick those tits! Give that woman some T.L.C. and you will see how great sex can really be!

Desire. If she doesn't want to have these orgasms, and if she's not willing to go for it, it's just not going to happen.

PHIL, AGE 24

I read the book in a couple of hours the day before I went to Las Vegas with my girlfriend.

During the drive there, I mentioned to her that I might want to try out some new sex stuff that I had read about. She said that would be fine, and that was that. We forgot about it.

How long have you two been together?

We've been together for over a year.

So we got to the hotel, went up to the room, and got into bed. I undressed her completely and took off all my clothes, too, and I tried to remember as much of the stuff I had read that I could.

I got her relaxed, and massaged her legs, and turned her over, and everything, like it said in the book.

I was worried about it, because she's kind of uptight sexually. But she was really into everything I was doing, and I kept reassuring her and holding her—hugging her—and amazingly, after about fifteen minutes, I started to recognize the signs.

Her vagina started expanding and contracting. And then she got really wet, and I thought to myself, "Wow, here it comes." And then, boom, there it was.

She asked me if I felt it, and of course I did. And the insides of her thighs were dripping wet.

We had plans to meet up with her brother and sister-in-law, so we had to stop after just once. But after dinner we went back to the room, and the next time we tried it was just so much easier. She came three times. It was really hot.

Why only three?

Well, the third time I had my dick inside her, and she came with me inside, and it felt *awesome.* Then I came, and that was it.

So this really works—just like it says in the book?

Pretty much just like it says. It was amazing. I'm sure we're going to do this every time from now on. She's just blown away by it.

How so?

Well, it seems to me it's a lot more intense. I mean, she's never gotten so wild in bed before.

BRIAN, AGE 28

I decided to try the technique with a girl I had never slept with before.

Her name was Nancy. I met her at a party, and when I met her I asked what she liked to do, and she said, "Get stoned and have sex."

Great.

So I hooked up with her about a week later. It was Memorial Day. She was house-sitting down in Palos Verdes, in this killer spread.

I went over there for a party session. There was

a party going on, we were drinking, smoking, and playing music.

Everyone bailed, and Nancy and I just started kissing.

There was a really good vibe between us. The kissing was really good, it felt really comfortable, she had a really nice body, very smooth, very warm—a very beautiful body.

The concept of a new kind of sex is neat, because it got me into the concept of foreplay again, instead of just, like, poke and choke.

Foreplay, cool.

We were on this killer couch, with end pieces and extensions, and huge. Romper-room style. You could be chasing each other from one end of the couch to the other.

So I'm massaging her body and touching her arms. I gave her a little back rub. Then I'm stroking her stomach, just south of her belly button, but north of any pubic hair. Then I was fingering her, and I was actually just going along with one finger, and I remembered that Tommy sometimes uses two fingers, so then I had two fingers going.

I was holding her tight. She wasn't going anywhere. I was using my left arm as leverage as well as my right, and I noticed it's a good bicep workout. And your forearms get a workout too. I had her cradled, and I was pulling her in with my left and pulling up with my right.

She was very wet, and she was actually a quiet girl, so it got very quiet for a while. But she was loving it, and I knew she was about to come. I didn't know if she was going to have an ejaculation, but she was getting really wet.

I repositioned my fingers a couple times, and it was definitely a workout. She reached a point, finally, where the fluid that was coming out of her was definitely a different viscosity—thinner, wetter. We kept going, and she didn't groan or anything, but her lower back started to arch up, and I applied a little bit more pressure, yet still tried to keep it fairly constant on her, and she just let go.

She came. She ejaculated. There were wet spots all over the couch. It was actually kind of funny. We had been in the pool, so we had towels around to clean up.

And she had never done that?

Never.

Then she said to me, "Oh, that was amazing."

I'm like, "Really? Why? Why was that so good?"

And she's like, "That just came from the deepest part of me I've ever experienced."

Did she know that she had actually squirted at that point?

I don't think so. I knew she was kind of embarrassed or not into that, so I didn't get into it with her.

She must have noticed!

I think she did, but she didn't really want to get into it.

That was the first time. Maybe it was just the position I was in, but it was a good, strong hold. The cradle.

Tell me about the other experience you had with female ejaculations.

It was actually before Nancy. I was house-sitting with Tracy.

But you said that was the first one you'd had.

The first time with *Nancy*. And it was the first time I was with her.

It was her first ejaculation and the first time you were with her.

Right.

And she said it came from the deepest part within her that she had ever felt.

But the first time I ever did it was with a different girl. It was with Tracy, house-sitting in Brentwood.

They had this great bed.

Tracy and I had been partying, rocking and rolling; she looked hot, she had the lingerie going. I was totally psyched.

Now, it was interesting, because I think that sexually she's always a challenge because she does have low self-esteem about her sexuality. She doesn't think that she's beautiful, she doesn't think that she has a beautiful body, she doesn't think that her pussy tastes good—none of that. Even though I tell her the opposite.

So I think that for her to really let go and enjoy herself is always something that makes me feel good. It's always a good accomplishment.

I basically did the same thing with Tracy as I did with Nancy, except I didn't have her cradled. I was more lying down next to her. And I was kissing her. I didn't kiss Nancy, but I kissed Tracy on her shoulders.

I spent a lot more time with Tracy just touching certain parts of her body with the back of my finger-nails, the middle of her chest between her breasts, down her stomach, above the pubic area, along the inner thighs.

And her nipples. She has very sensitive nipples. She was getting extremely wet.

I went in there with one finger, probing around.

Then I put in two fingers and continued to work at it, to find that spot.

Going upward, per the instructions.

I was actually getting into the visualization process of imagining where my fingers were.

I remember being really turned on.

I felt her getting really wet, but she came right away.

Really?

By the time I had my fingers inside of her, maybe three to five minutes. But I'd spent more time touching certain parts of her body, plus, she was a very excitable girl.

Like I said, I had two fingers up there, I had the visualization going, and I could feel her getting really wet.

Then she came. She's much more vocal when we're making love. She groans, and she'll say she's going to come.

She came and she squirted.

It actually hit me in the arm. It hit my arm, and I'm not sure where the rest went. It hit me on the underside of my arm, from my forearm all the way to near my elbow.

What was her reaction to the situation?

She told me afterward that it was the best orgasm she'd ever had.

Was she aware of what happened?

I didn't sense that she was, and I didn't bring it up.

Both these women seem to be a little sensitive about their sexuality, so I didn't want to make a big deal about this.

But they both expressed to me that this had been something unique in their sexual experiences. Something unique had just happened to them.

And they both said that the orgasms came from a deeper part of their body. They came from a place they had never felt before.

Tracy said it was like an earthquake.

She said, "I had pre-shock tremors. I had an earthquake. And I had all these aftershocks."

MEDICAL OPINION AND EVALUATION BY STUART J. GLASSMAN, M.D.

I have read *Secrets of Sensual Lovemaking,* and I was very impressed by some of the ideas that the book brings up. The interplay between physical and psychological sexual arousal is quite accurate and brings up one of the key concerns of the '90s. AIDS has caused sex to now be very anxiety-provoking, and Mr. Leonardi's techniques may help to lessen the anxiety. Digital vaginal stimulation is less likely to cause transmission of HIV, provided that there are no open cuts or sores on the finger. Always be aware that transmission can go both ways. But these techniques seem to allow for pleasurable sex with a minimal risk of HIV transmission, which may help relieve anxiety and put trust and enjoyment back into human sexuality.

FINAL WORDS

WHO'S DOING WHO?

It's amazing. I'll talk to a guy and he'll say, "I met this girl at a party last night, and I got her," or "I fucked her," or "I did this or that," as if he is this incredible person who convinced this girl to give herself up to him.

If I ask him what happened, he'll probably say, "I saw her, thought she was hot, and went over to talk to her. And I did her."

If I ask him, "Did you ever stop to think that

maybe she did *you*?" Almost invariably, the guy will say, "What do you mean, *'She did me'*?"

"Isn't it possible that that woman noticed you *first* and said to her friend, 'That guy is hot—I'd do him. I'd fuck him.' Someone had to see someone first."

Every time, the guy will say, "No way. Women don't think like that. Women don't talk like that."

Bullshit they don't.

Just as most guys aren't going to walk up to a woman if they're not attracted to her, women certainly aren't going to go home with you or have sex with you if they're not turned on by you.

What it comes down to is this: If you meet a woman and it's obvious that you two are attracted to each other, there's nothing "right" you can do from here on; all you can do is fuck it up. And that's what a lot of people do.

WHO'S DOING WHO 2?

I guarantee you if you asked a thousand men and a thousand women, randomly, how many people they've each slept with, the numbers for each sex would not be equal. With a sample size that large, the numbers *have* to be equal, but they won't be.

It's amazing. If you ask men how many women they've slept with they'd say, "15, 20, 30, 40, 100, 200," and so on.

And if you ask women how many men they've slept with, they'll say, "9, 7, 4, 8, 12."

Guys will overexaggerate because "getting laid" a lot is something to brag about.

But women will understate the amount of men they've been with.

Come on!

Who's doing who?

There aren't enough promiscuous women in this world to make up for all these guys who claim to get laid so often. Someone's lying.

WHO ARE <u>YOU</u> DOING?

If you don't appreciate the person you're having sex with as a person—if she's purely a sex object—then you're missing the point.

I'm not saying you have to love that person or even be in a long-term relationship with her. I'm just saying you should make an effort to get to know her as a person, to get a feel for what she likes in life (not just what she does for a living—that's not necessarily who she is).

Find out what makes her laugh—what pisses

her off—what makes her react—and you'll find yourself getting to know a lot more people and appreciating the remarkable diversity of human-kind.

GOALS

Women will enjoy themselves tremendously if you don't have what I would call the "Vagina Goal."

Most guys kiss a woman so that they can then touch her breasts. Then—like in high school—hopefully she'll let him touch her butt. And if she lets him touch her butt, hopefully she'll let him touch the front of her pants. And then hopefully he'll be able to get his hand down her pants.

What amazes me is that your typical thirty-five-year-old man is trying to do the same thing—trying to get as far as he can! Because ultimately his goal is . . . the vagina.

He wants to get to the vagina!

You might say, "Well, if you don't get to the vagina, how's she going to have any fun?" Of course, she's not necessarily going to have the best time, but that should come naturally. A good way to look at it is this:

When you're with a woman, don't expect any-thing.

If you were playing softball and you expected to get a hit every time, it would rarely happen. But it will happen often enough when you aren't trying so hard. It works like that in anything. So be at ease with women.

If you're putting pressure on yourself, you're not acting like yourself. And women see right through that. Many women have been with enough guys who grope and grab to recognize another groper and grabber. Within no time, they'll know if a guy is hoping to get as far as he can—and, of course, not actually enjoying what he's doing with her—he's just patting himself on the back for every base that he touches!

WHY ARE MEN'S ORGASMS
MORE IMPORTANT?

Actually, they're not. But everybody, including you—man or woman—treats them as if they are.

Think about the last time you had sex more than once in an evening. How many times was it? 2, 3, 4, or more?

And how did you determine this number?

Simple. It was the number of times that you (if you're a man) or your lover (if you're a woman) came during intercourse!

Why is it that if a man comes twice and a woman comes five times during sex, they've had sex *twice*?

And if the man comes five times and the woman doesn't come at all, they've still had sex *five times.*

Now, imagine if a woman friend came up to you and said, "I had sex twelve times last night."

You'd immediately say, "Wow! He came twelve times?"

But if she said, "No. *I* came twelve times."

"That doesn't count," you'd tell her. "How many times did *he* come?"

So, why are men's orgasms more important than women's orgasms? I don't think they are; maybe they won't be, once more women start ejaculating. . . .

TRUST YOUR INSTINCTS

Every so often, a woman will meet someone and she'll just *know* that she's met a great lover.

If she goes to bed with this man, she's not necessarily looking for him to be her boyfriend or husband. She just knows that she is going to have a wonderful time.

Sex is a natural function. It's a natural desire.

Some people will disagree and say it's only a reproductive function, but come on—who are they trying to kid? Although I was raised Catholic, I don't believe that for a second.

Most women are in touch with that natural function and most men are not. To allow yourself to be natural—in other words, to be instinctive—is a very female thing to do.

People will talk about "women's intuition." I don't think only women have intuition and men don't. Men are *afraid* of intuition. They're afraid to use their instincts, to follow their gut.

Most women are not afraid to use their instincts. And, as stated before, women enjoy sex; most men don't.

EVERY TRICK IN THE BOOK

I've heard complaints from women who've said: "This guy knew every trick in the book, but he didn't express himself. He was completely quiet. He didn't make any noise. His body didn't move much, except when he was actually having sex with me. He didn't seem to be turned on. He loved giving me pleasure, but it didn't seem to turn him on."

Women want to see their lovers turned on as much as men who really enjoy sex care about having their lovers turned on.

The greatest sex occurs when two people are

1. turned on by giving the other person pleasure
2. not afraid to express their own pleasure.

If this works both ways, an endless erotic cycle develops.

WHY DON'T WOMEN
HAVE MORE SEX?

It's a lot easier for a woman to get sex than it is for a man to get sex. Now why is that?

Some women claim they can't find a lover or that they can't meet men. But what they're really saying is that they can't find the *right* lover or the *right* man. And after women realize that 95% of men are not good lovers or are just assholes, women understandably become gun-shy.

Most women don't have sex as often as they could, while most men wish they could have more sex than they do. For men, it's a problem of not having enough opportunities. For women, there just aren't enough *quality* opportunities.

And it all goes back to the fact that men don't enjoy sex. If they did, there would be many more quality opportunities for women.

CAN A WOMAN COME FROM KISSING?

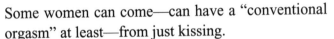

Some women can come—can have a "conventional orgasm" at least—from just kissing.

Yes, it's happened to me. And what's funny is that when it happened to a woman I was with, she apologized to me. She thought she was weird. (Unusual? Yes! Weird? No!)

She later admitted that her friends were jealous; they had enough trouble having orgasms when guys were going down on them, and this woman was complaining because she could do it when she was kissing. Her friends said, "Are you kidding? You're the luckiest woman in the world."

PRELIMINARY EYE CONTACT

When you're talking to someone you're attracted to, maintain eye contact with them.

If anything's a turnoff, it's someone looking away from you as you talk to them.

Here's the scenario: You meet someone for the first time, and you think that they're into you. You talk to them, but then they start looking away.

Is it because the person's not interested? Or is he or she just being insecure? Either way, it's such a distraction.

Have the confidence—or force yourself—when

you're meeting or talking to someone to look into their eyes. Force yourself.

If that person feels intimidated by you, not to worry, because that person probably isn't someone who's ready to let himself or herself go anyway.

TO DATE OR NOT TO DATE

Many people, while on a date, approach the "date" differently from "other" situations.

I don't. When I go out with a woman for the first time, I NEVER look at it like I'm going on a date. I only go out with a woman because I, simply, would like to go somewhere with her. She's someone with whom I'd like to spend some time, just as I would with a friend.

I look at a woman as a possible future friend.

People might say, "How do you know who you want to spend time with?"

That's what I'm talking about when I say to use your instincts. It's a tool that you can hone. Just trust that tool inside of you.

If there's a woman you'd like to spend some time with, just say that to her. "We should get together soon. What are you doing later?"

Don't make it a date. Just be straightforward.

Sure, there's something to be said about dates and being romantic, but usually with someone you don't know that well, you just have to go with your gut feelings. If not, you'll be on another dreaded, contrived "date."

Blah!

I've heard too many women say, "I went on a date with this guy, and he's really nice and everything, but there just wasn't any spark." They were probably thinking more about what a date should be like rather than having a good time. The few times that I've been out with a woman and the word *date* even came up were times when the women commented on how enjoyable it was to be out with a man and *not feel like they were out on a date.*

When on a date you're kind of nervous, you're kind of uptight. You're worried about how you look or how you feel or what you're saying. Those thoughts never cross my mind on a date. Don't let them cross yours either.

SUPPLY AND DEMAND

I was telling someone about this book, and she asked, "If this technique works so well, why would Tom want to share it with other men?" Here's a partial answer:

Supply and demand.

There is probably no greater demand for and so little supply of anything in this world as there is for great male lovers.

If I could spend all my waking hours for the next fifty years having sex with women, I would still have made no visible dent in the number of women in this world who are not having good sex lives.

No one person could ever cater to the desires of all the women out there. And I don't think thousands of men could. There's just an incredible dearth of men who don't know what the hell they're doing!

I hope I've helped!

FURTHER READING

These are books I came across when I was about thirteen because my mother happened to have them around the house.

My Secret Garden by Nancy Friday (Pocket Books)

The Hite Report by Shere Hite (Dell Publishing)

The New Our Bodies, Our Selves by the Boston Women's Health Book Collective (Touchstone)

These are books about female sexuality, and from them I learned about sex from a woman's perspective.

I really don't think men need to know about male sexuality. It's a natural thing. You know how to have sex. You know what you can do with yourself, what feels good to you.

What you want to know is with whom you are having sex. Learn about the women you're going to be with! You'll read these books and you might think, "My God—I can't believe women think like this." But they do! They *all* do.

You'll begin to realize after reading this stuff that women think about sex too. They have fantasies that aren't necessarily just fantasies but perhaps *goals* that they would act out on if they found themselves in the right situation. Get the hint? You'll no longer look at women as sex objects—but rather as *sexual beings with whom you can share erotic pleasure!*